W9-CRU-585

Women in Profile

Rebels

Carlotta Hacker

Crabtree Publishing Company

Dedication

This series is dedicated to every woman who has followed her dreams and to every young girl who hopes to do the same. While overcoming great odds and often oppression, the remarkable women in this series have triumphed in their fields. Their dedication, hard work, and excellence can serve as an inspiration to all—young and old, male and female. Women in Profile is both an acknowledgment of and a tribute to these great women.

Project Coordinator
Leslie Strudwick
Crabtree Editor
Virginia Mainprize
Editing and Proofreading
Alana Luft
Krista McLuskey
Lauri Seidlitz
Design
Warren Clark

Published by Crabtree Publishing Company

350 Fifth Avenue, Suite 3308
New York, NY
USA 10018

360 York Road, R.R. 4
Niagara-on-the-Lake
Ontario, Canada
L0S 1J0

Copyright © 1999 WEIGL EDUCATIONAL PUBLISHERS LIMITED. All rights reserved. No part of this publication may be reproduced, stored in a retrieval system, or transmitted in any form or by any means, electronic, mechanical, photocopying, recording, or otherwise, without the prior written permission of Weigl Educational Publishers Limited.

Cataloging-in-Publication Data

Hacker, Carlotta.
      Rebels / Carlotta Hacker.
                 p. cm — (Women in profile)
      Includes bibliographical references and index.
      Summary. Chronicles the lives and achievements of revolutionary women, including civil rights activist Angela Davis, human rights activist Rigoberta Menchú, and suffragist Emmeline Pankhurst.
      ISBN 0-7787-0014-3 (rlb). — ISBN 0-7787-0036-4 (pbk.)
      1. Women heroes—Biography—Juvenile literature. [1. Heroes. 2. Women—Biography.] I. Title. II. Series.
CT3207.H33   1999
920.72—dc21
[B]   98-40367
                                                CIP
                                                AC

Photograph Credits
Every reasonable effort has been made to trace ownership and to obtain permission to reprint copyright material. The publishers would be pleased to have any errors or omissions brought to their attention so that they may be corrected in subsequent printings.

Agence France Presse/Corbis-Bettmann: page 32; Archive Photos: cover, pages 7, 8, 10, 12, 14, 23, 26, 27, 28, 34, 35, 38, 42, 43; Canapress Photo Service: pages 6, 24, 29, 33; Corbis-Bettmann: pages 37, 40; Green Belt Movement: pages 18, 21, 22; Image Works: page 44 (Michael Schwarz); National Archives of Canada: page 45 (C-9480); Reuters/Corbis-Bettmann: page 30; UN/DPI: page 20; UPI/Corbis-Bettmann: pages 9, 11, 15, 16, 17, 36, 39, 41.

Contents

More Women in Profile

Rebels

W hat is a rebel? One definition is "a person who refuses to obey those in authority." People rebel for many reasons and in many different ways. Someone who refuses to join a gang could be called a rebel. So could the leader of the gang. The best definition might be that a rebel is someone who has strong beliefs and the courage to act on his or her beliefs, no matter what other people think or do.

In other words, you do not have to start a revolution to be a rebel. You certainly do not have to use violence. You simply have to believe in something very strongly and then take action.

Many rebels have taken action to help others. They have fought against laws that treat some people unfairly. They have opposed harsh and cruel governments. Some rebels have spent their lives trying to change things. Some have even died for their cause.

Women, both alone and in groups, have rebelled against many things throughout history. Some of the bravest were those who broke with tradition and tried to improve the lives of all women, by getting them the right to vote, for example.

This book tells you about a few of the many rebels who have helped bring about change. You may be able to think of others. Because such women have dared to rebel, life has improved today for many people, both men and women.

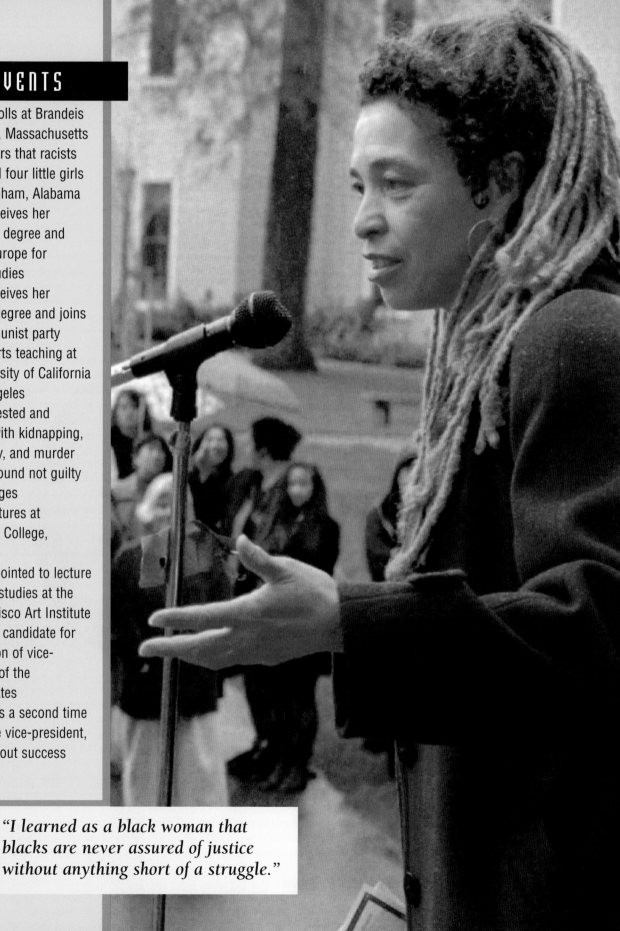

"I learned as a black woman that blacks are never assured of justice without anything short of a struggle."

Angela Davis

American Political Activist

Early Years

"No, you can't go in. We are in a hurry," said Angela's mother as they walked past Kiddyland. She did not want to tell her children that the fun fair was for whites only. In the 1940s, there was no Kiddyland for African-American children in Birmingham, Alabama. As Angela grew older, she learned that many other things were not for African-American children.

Her family lived in a nice part of Birmingham, but some people wanted it to be an all-white neighborhood. Sometimes, during the night, they threw bombs at the houses of African-Americans living there. So many bombs went off that the area was nicknamed "Dynamite Hill."

Angela went to a segregated school, where all of the students were African American. Some of the children did not have warm clothing or money for lunch. Angela worked hard and received good grades. Her father was pleased that she was setting a good example for her younger sister and two brothers.

The laws that segregated African Americans in the United States no longer exist.

BACKGROUNDER

Segregation

When Angela was a child, African Americans in the southern United States were segregated (separated) from other Americans. African Americans could not go to white people's schools. They had to live in different parts of town and travel on a different part of the bus. They were not allowed to eat in the same restaurants as white people. Segregation was the law in Alabama and all the southern states.

Quick Notes

- Angela's parents, Frank and Sallye Davis, were both teachers.

- Angela's father gave up teaching to run his own garage.

- Angela has written several books, including: *If They Come in the Morning* (1971), *Women, Race, and Class* (1983), *Angela Davis: An Autobiography* (1988), and *Women, Culture, and Politics* (1989).

Developing Skills

A ngela's mother took her children to New York City almost every summer. Angela loved New York City. There was no segregation because the city was in a northern state. Angela could eat in any restaurant or swim at any public beach. She could go to all sorts of places where white people went.

When Angela was fifteen, she won a scholarship to a private school in New York City. She was thrilled to get away from Birmingham's **racism**. After graduating in 1961, she won a scholarship to Brandeis University in Massachusetts. She spent her third year of university in France, at the University of Paris.

In Paris, Angela met students from Algeria, a country in North Africa, which was then a **colony** of France. The students told her how Algerians were trying to free themselves from French rule. Angela was fascinated by these stories. It seemed to her that the French treated Algerians the same way the whites at home treated African Americans.

Soon after Angela returned to the United States, white racists threw a bomb into an African-American church in Birmingham. The bomb landed among the Sunday-school children and killed four little girls. Angela knew three of them.

Angela's experiences at home and in France made her determined to bring about change.

Angela was furious with the whites who had killed the girls. She was furious with the people who made laws against African Americans. She was determined to do something to change things. Her mother was active in the civil rights movement, led by the great African-American minister, Dr. Martin Luther King, Jr. The aim of the civil rights movement was to get laws changed so that African Americans would be treated the same as whites throughout the United States. Angela, too, supported the non-violent civil rights movement, but she was not sure that it could end segregation.

While studying for her master's degree, Angela made friends with the Black Panthers. She did not agree with all of their ideas. After much thought, Angela decided that only **communism** could bring the type of change that was needed to improve the lives of African Americans. In 1968, she joined the Communist party.

BACKGROUNDER

The Black Panthers

The Black Panther Party for Self-Defense was formed in 1966 to protect African-American communities from unfair police activity. The Panthers believed a revolution was needed to change society. Dressed in black and wearing black berets, the Panthers carried guns, which led to several shootouts with police. In the early 1970s, some Panther party members ran in elections and began community programs, such as food giveaways and health clinics. Many bright, young African Americans, including Angela Davis, were attracted to the party during the 1960s and 1970s. Angela, and many other women, later left the Panthers because they felt the party did not support an equal role for African-American women.

Angela often spoke to crowds of thousands, urging them to fight racism.

"I am constantly being asked why I decided to join the Communist party. It isn't something in my own personal development. It's for the development of black people."

BACKGROUNDER

The Appeal of Communism

Communism is a form of government in which everyone is supposed to be equal. It owes its origins to two Germans, Karl Marx and Friedrich Engels, who wrote *The Communist Manifesto* (1848). The last words of the manifesto are "Workers of the world, unite! You have nothing to lose but your chains." Many people have been attracted to communism because they think it will free them from the "chains" of having to work long hours for low pay. They hope that under a communist system children will no longer go hungry, and there will be free health care and other benefits.

Accomplishments

In 1969, Angela began to teach at the University of California at Los Angeles (UCLA). Soon afterward, a newspaper reported that she was a member of the Communist party. She was fired from her job. She fought back and was allowed to continue teaching, but she was not hired again the following year. This was partly because she had become an **activist** for the party.

Angela was fighting racism in her own way, giving fiery speeches that drew huge crowds. She was a strong supporter of two African-American communists who were in Soledad Prison in California. One of them, George Jackson, was killed by guards in 1970. They said he had been trying to escape, but Angela did not believe them.

Angela's support of the Soledad prisoners angered some people so much that they threatened to kill her. To protect herself, she bought several guns. These guns were taken by Angela's friend Jonathan, George Jackson's brother. He used them to try to rescue a prisoner who was being tried at the county courthouse. There was a shootout, and several people were killed, including Jonathan and the judge.

Supporters from as far away as New Delhi, India, joined to demand Angela's release.

As soon as Angela heard of the shooting, she went into hiding. She knew the police would never believe she was innocent because guns registered in her name were found at the courthouse. Sure enough, she was named one of the "ten most-wanted criminals" in the United States. Two months later, she was caught and charged with plotting murder.

While Angela was in prison waiting for her trial, people all over the world rallied in her support. Protest marches were held in places as far away as India. Back home, the words "Free Angela" appeared on everything from billboards to buttons. At her trial in 1972, the jury found Angela not guilty.

In the following months, Angela toured the United States and other countries. People considered her a hero. After her tour, she continued her teaching career. Over the years, she has taught and lectured at Stanford University, Claremont College, the San Francisco Art Institute, and many other places.

"I believe that under the categories Marx developed you can get to the roots of racism— what it's all about and what you have to do to destroy it."

Angela has continued to fight racism wherever she finds it, and she has remained a member of the Communist party. In 1980 and again in 1984, Angela tried unsuccessfully to get elected as the communist candidate for the position of vice-president of the United States.

Following her release from prison, Angela continued to spread her message. She gave speeches and taught at colleges and universities.

"The more I learned about socialism, the more reconciled I was to life, which I no longer saw as a swamp but as a battlefield."

Dolores Ibarruri

Spanish Political Leader and Revolutionary

Early Years

Dolores was born in Gallarta, a mining town in northern Spain. One of her earliest memories was the constant sound of trains from the mine rattling along the rails near her home. Dolores hated the mines. The dust and mud got into everything. Each night, her father and brothers came home from work covered with dirt. Dolores's knuckles were red and raw from scrubbing their clothes clean.

Dolores's parents sent her to the local school, where she was taught to read and write. She was also taught to be a Catholic, but she turned against religion as she grew older. The priests said that the rich should help the poor, yet none of the rich people in Gallarta were doing so. When Dolores's father and other miners went on **strike** for better pay, the priests sided with the mine owners.

BACKGROUNDER

Life in the Mines

There were rich deposits of iron ore and other minerals in northern Spain. Thousands of people worked in the mines, but the pay was low and the work was hard. The miners chipped out the minerals with picks and drills or blew up the rock with dynamite. Many were killed in the explosions. When a miner was too old for such hard work, he was given an even worse job. Standing knee-deep in mud all day, he washed the crumbled ore and separated it from the earth. Other equally hard jobs were done by boys as young as ten years old, or by women.

FRANCE

Gallarta

SPAIN

PORTUGAL

MEDITERRANEAN SEA

Developing Skills

Dolores left school when she was fifteen and started to train as a teacher, but she never finished the course. The cost was more than she could afford. She worked for a time as a maid, then she got a job she liked better, selling sardines. These small fish were plentiful in the sea around northern Spain. Dolores carried the fish from village to village on a huge tray, which she balanced on her head.

In 1916, Dolores married a miner. He was a member of the **socialist** movement, which wanted to form a government that would give working people more rights. Dolores became a socialist, too.

When she heard that working people had seized power in Russia and set up a communist government, Dolores was thrilled. **Communism** was more extreme than socialism, but Dolores thought the system might work well in Spain. She was among the first to join the Communist Party of Spain when it was formed in 1920.

After a revolution in 1917, the communists took control of the government in Russia. Russia was renamed the Soviet Union.

"My grandfather died in a mine, crushed by a block of ore.... The miners' life was hard even when they were in the prime of life, and it became unbearable and inhuman when they were old."

During the following years, Dolores became one of Spain's most active communists. She attended Communist party meetings in Spain and in other countries. She made passionate speeches, calling for a change of government. She worked as an editor of the communist newspaper, *Mundo Obrero* (Worker's World), and wrote many articles about communism. Dolores signed her articles "La Pasionaria" (the Passion Flower). Soon, people throughout the country were talking about La Pasionaria.

Not everyone supported Dolores's work. She was accused of trying to **overthrow** the government because she was encouraging the workers to rebel. She was imprisoned several times. When the Communist party was banned by a new **right-wing** government, Dolores's life became even more difficult. Dolores and her friends could now meet only in secret. When she wanted to attend a conference in the Soviet Union, she had to get out of Spain secretly. She walked across the Pyrenees mountain range.

Communists from many different countries attended the conference. During the meeting, they formed a committee to make decisions about things that concerned them all. Dolores was elected a member of this committee.

BACKGROUNDER

La Pasionaria

Dolores was a tall and dignified woman with flashing brown eyes. She always dressed in black. A brilliant public speaker, she could hold an audience spellbound. One moment, she would have everyone listening to her words. The next moment, they would be cheering wildly as she roused them to action. Many people thought of her as the "living embodiment of fighting, suffering Spain."

Dolores had a powerful effect on the crowds she addressed.

BACKGROUNDER

The Spanish Civil War

In 1931, the King of Spain was forced off his throne, and Spain was declared "a democratic **republic** of all workers and classes." The republic was not a success. So many political parties wanted power that no government was able to stay in office for long. By the end of 1935, there had been twenty-eight different governments. In the 1936 elections, several left-wing parties joined together to form a group called the Popular Front. This group won the election, but its government was very unpopular with the wealthier classes, and fighting broke out between the Popular Front and right-wing forces. This conflict brought on the Spanish Civil War (1936–39) in which the right-wing forces, led by General Francisco Franco, fought the left-wing forces, known as republicans. Franco's army won the war, and he became head of the new Spanish government.

In 1936, Dolores traveled to Paris with her delegation to discuss the troubles in Spain.

Accomplishments

In 1936, the right-wing government in Spain fell from power, and the Communist party became legal again. It became a leading member of the **left-wing** group of parties called the Popular Front, which won the 1936 election. Seventeen communists were elected to the Cortés, the Spanish parliament. Dolores was one of them.

In June that year, Dolores made a speech in the Cortés in which she attacked the former right-wing government. She accused its leaders of plotting to overthrow the Popular Front. Those political leaders should be arrested, she said, and so should some of the wealthy landlords. There were riots in many parts of the country, and some landowners were turned off their lands.

One month later, General Franco led the Spanish army in revolt against the Popular Front. This event began the Spanish Civil War. Speaking on the radio that evening, Dolores called on the people to fight Franco's forces. "It is better to die on your feet than live on your knees," she said. "They shall not pass!"

"It is better to die on your feet than live on your knees!"

Many Spanish people were killed during the next few years, as the war spread across the country. Dolores was very busy during these terrible times. She helped set up hospitals for the wounded and visited soldiers, giving them encouragement. She helped hand out food to **refugee** children. She also made speeches. All this time, she continued her work as a member of the Cortés, which still governed part of Spain. She served as vice-president from 1937 until General Franco and his supporters won the war in 1939.

After General Franco took control of the government in Spain, Dolores fled to France. She later settled in the Soviet Union. From there, she made radio broadcasts to Spain, calling on the people to overthrow General Franco. She never stopped working for Spanish communism.

In 1977, two years after General Franco died, the Communist party was again made legal in Spain. Dolores returned home and was elected to the Cortés, although she was eighty-two years old. She soon found the work too much and had to resign. She lived for another twelve years as one of Spain's most honored citizens.

Quick Notes

- **Dolores had six children (including triplets), but all except two of them died during childhood.**

- **The Spanish phrase for "They shall not pass!" is "*No pasaran!*" It was the battle cry of the republican forces in the civil war.**

- **In the novel *For Whom the Bell Tolls*, American author Ernest Hemingway is said to have based his character Pilar on La Pasionaria.**

Dolores was elected to parliament, even though she was over eighty years old.

"When any of us feel she has an idea or an opportunity, she should go ahead and do it.... One person can make a difference."

Wangari Maathai

Kenyan Activist and Environmentalist

Early Years

Wangari grew up in the highlands of Kenya, where her parents had a farm. It was just a small farm, but it produced enough food to feed the family's six children. As the oldest girl, Wangari was busy looking after her younger brothers and sisters, but her parents made sure she went to school. They had great ambitions for her.

Wangari did not disappoint her parents. She did so well at school that in the early 1960s, she won a scholarship to go to university in the United States. There she received a degree in biology from a college in Kansas. She then enrolled at the University of Pittsburgh to study for a master's degree.

After receiving her master's degree, Wangari could have looked for a job in the United States, but she returned to Kenya. "I had promised to make a contribution to my country," she said.

BACKGROUNDER

Kenya

Kenya was a British **colony** before it gained independence in 1963. Although Kenya lies on the equator, most of the country is on a high plateau where the climate is very pleasant. The Kenyan highlands are known for their excellent farmland. There are also spectacular game reserves where visitors can watch lions and other wild animals.

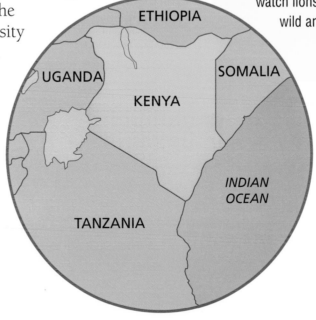

ETHIOPIA

UGANDA

SOMALIA

KENYA

INDIAN OCEAN

TANZANIA

BACKGROUNDER

Trees and the Environment

Deforestation has become an urgent environmental problem around the world. Especially in areas with large populations, forests are cut down for firewood and to make more space for farmland. This leads to long-term environmental change. Forests add oxygen and water to the air. When forests are cut down, less rain falls, causing drier, hotter climates. Tree roots hold soil in place. They prevent soil from blowing away in the wind or washing away in heavy rains. In areas that have lost their trees, deserts often develop in what was once rich land full of plants and animals.

Developing Skills

Wangari continued her education after coming home, and in 1971, she earned a Ph.D. from the University of Nairobi in Kenya. She got a good teaching job at the university, but many men who did not have a Ph.D were upset. They thought it was wrong that a woman was better educated than they were.

Two years before, Wangari had married, and in the early 1970s, her husband ran for parliament. He promised the unemployed that he would find them jobs. After he was elected, Wangari made great efforts to see that this promise was kept. Many people found work with her help.

Wangari also helped the people of Kenya in other ways. She realized that many families in the countryside went hungry because they had no way of cooking their food. They did not have electricity, and because all the trees had been cut down, there was no firewood. Wangari's answer was to grow trees. This project would improve the environment and provide firewood. It would also give jobs to the people who grew and planted the trees.

Wangari's tree-planting project helped to repair damage caused by deforestation.

On World Environment Day, June 5, 1977, Wangari and her friends planted the first trees of a project called the Green Belt Movement (GBM). "We started with seven trees in a small park in Nairobi," she said. Before long, thousands of trees were being planted all over the country.

The GBM workers grew the trees as **seedlings** and gave them to anyone who would plant them. As news of the project spread, donations of money poured in from as far away as Canada. By the 1990s, GBM was employing thousands of Kenyan women in more than a thousand tree farms. People across the country were asking how they could get seedlings. More than ten million trees were planted.

Wangari's marriage was not going as well as her tree-planting project. Her husband was jealous of her success, and he divorced her in the early 1980s. Wangari did not want a divorce. At her divorce trial, she accused the judges of siding with her husband. To punish her for criticizing them, the judges sentenced her to six months in jail, but she was released after three days.

Quick Notes

- Wangari has two sons and a daughter.

- In 1993, Wangari visited the United States to give talks about environmental problems.

- Wangari was the first woman to earn a Ph.D. degree at the University of Nairobi. She was also the first woman to be a senior lecturer, the first to be an associate professor, and the first to be head of a department.

- Wangari grew up in an area of Kenya called the White Highlands. This region became famous because of a book written by Isak Dinesen, called *Out of Africa*.

"The Green Belt Movement is about hope. It tells people that they are responsible for their own lives. It suggests that, at the very least, you can plant a tree and improve your habitat."

BACKGROUNDER

President Moi

Since 1978, Kenya has been ruled by President Daniel arap Moi, who made the country a one-party state. Although people could elect members to parliament, all the members had to belong to President Moi's political party, so he was always re-elected. In 1991, President Moi unwillingly agreed to allow other parties to exist. This promise did not bring a change of government. Anyone who dared to stand against the president ran the risk of being harmed. In January 1998, President Moi began a fifth term as Kenya's ruler.

Accomplishments

After her divorce, Wangari quit her job at the University of Nairobi so she could run for parliament. When she failed to get elected, she tried to go back to her job, but the university would not accept her. Many of the men there had never forgiven her for getting a Ph.D. when they did not have one. Some also disapproved because she was not behaving as they thought a Kenyan woman should. In their view, a woman should do as she was told; she should not take the lead.

Wangari took the lead again in 1989, when the government decided to build a sixty-two-story skyscraper in Nairobi's main park. Not only would this huge building ruin the park, but it would cost $200 million, which the country could not afford. Wangari's protests attracted support in other countries as well as in Kenya, and the plan had to be dropped. President Moi was furious, saying it was un-African for a woman to oppose a man.

Wangari organized women throughout Kenya to get involved in their communities.

From then on, Wangari and the president were openly in conflict. In 1992, she joined the Forum for the Restoration of Democracy, a political group working for greater freedoms for Kenyan people. Such groups had at last been permitted in Kenya, but the police harassed those who joined them. Wangari was often arrested for no reason at all and questioned for hours.

In 1992, Wangari joined a **hunger strike** to support a group of women whose sons had been imprisoned without trial. The police attacked the women and beat Wangari unconscious. Although she spent some time in the hospital and the police later broke into her house, she continued to support people who were treated unfairly. "If we cannot protect our own species," she said, "I don't know what we are doing protecting the tree species."

Wangari's work has won her many awards, including the Woman of the World Award (1983 and 1989) and the Africa Prize for Leadership for the Sustainable End to Hunger (1991). She has been called "the leading environmentalist on the African continent."

"I have had the fortune of breaking a lot of records—first woman this, first woman that—and I think that has created a lot of jealousy without me realizing it. Sometimes, we don't quite realize that not everybody is clapping when we're succeeding."

Wangari (left) and other women on the hunger strike chained themselves together as they marched to the courthouse.

"I'm not a socialist because of any high-flown theorizing. Life has made me one."

Key Events

1966 Enrolls at Queen's University, Belfast
1969 Writes *The Price of My Soul*
1969 Is elected to the British parliament
1975 Helps found the Irish Republican Socialist Party
1979 Runs, unsuccessfully, for the European parliament
1981 Is shot by terrorists
1982 Runs, unsuccessfully, for the parliament of the Republic of Ireland
1990 Tours the United States in support of the Birmingham Six

Bernadette Devlin McAliskey

Irish Civil Rights Activist

Early Years

Bernadette's father hated the English and dreamed of the day Northern Ireland would no longer be under their control. In the bedtime stories he read Bernadette as a child, the English were always the bad guys. They were the ones who bullied and lied and could never be trusted. Many of the stories were about things that had happened in Ireland hundreds of years before.

Bernadette's father, because he was so anti-English, had difficulty finding work. As a result, his large family never had enough money. They lived in Cookstown, a small market town in Northern Ireland where there was a lot of poverty and unemployment. Like their neighbors, the Devlins were Catholic.

When Bernadette was nine, her father died. The family had even less money, but the children never went hungry. Bernadette worked hard at school and won a scholarship to Queen's University in Belfast.

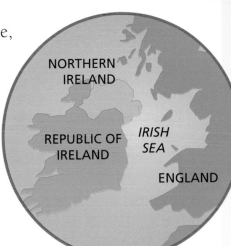

NORTHERN IRELAND

REPUBLIC OF IRELAND

IRISH SEA

ENGLAND

Backgrounder

Catholics and Protestants in Northern Ireland

Hundreds of years ago, the English invaded Ireland and made it part of the United Kingdom. The English and Scots who settled in Ireland were Protestant, while the original Irish were Catholic. The Irish wanted Ireland to be a separate country. In the 1920s, Britain gave way to Irish demands, and most of Ireland became independent. Only six northern counties remained part of the United Kingdom. Most of the people in Northern Ireland were Protestant. Most of the politicians and landlords were Protestant, and they made laws that favored their own group. The hatred between Protestants and Catholics grew, and there has been much violence between the two groups.

Developing Skills

Bernadette started at Queen's University in 1966. As well as attending lectures, she joined the debating society. She also became involved in the civil rights movement. The aim of this movement was to get fair treatment for all the **downtrodden** people of Northern Ireland, especially Catholics and low-income people. Bernadette knew, from her own experience, how the laws of the country made life very hard for Catholics.

> *"I went up to university with some vague notion of being able, one day, to improve some aspect of life in Northern Ireland."*

As a student, Bernadette knew that she had to do something to stop unfair treatment of the Catholics in Northern Ireland.

The civil rights movement held its first big rally in 1968, calling for reforms and social justice. The police responded by charging into the crowd. Bernadette watched in horror as a young man who was trying to protect her was pounded with a police baton. "I was so angry," she said, "that I went back to Queen's and poured it all out to the other students. I haven't stopped since."

Soon afterward, Bernadette helped form a student group called People's Democracy. The members of this group wanted to get the laws changed so that the police would have less power. They also wanted better housing for low-income families and a fairer system of hiring workers. Often, Protestants were hired instead of Catholics because most businesses were run by Protestants. This sort of thing should be forbidden by law, said Bernadette. All people should be treated equally.

As Bernadette organized more and more rallies, she became a hero to many people. She was known as "the five-foot **firebrand**." When an election was called for the Northern Ireland parliament in 1969, her friends persuaded Bernadette to run as a candidate. Bernadette failed to get elected, but she won many votes. This support encouraged her to try to get elected as a member of the British parliament later that year. She visited even the smallest country villages, giving speeches and reminding people how unfair many laws were. To the delight of her followers, she won the election.

Less than a week later, Bernadette arrived in parliament. She caused quite a stir, and not just because she was an **activist**. She was only twenty-one years old, the youngest woman ever to sit in the British parliament. Bernadette was also the youngest person (man or woman) to be a member of the British parliament in two hundred years.

BACKGROUNDER

Two Parliaments

When Bernadette first stood as a candidate, the people of Northern Ireland could elect members to two different parliaments. One was their own parliament in Belfast, which made laws affecting Northern Ireland. The other was the British parliament in London, which made laws affecting the entire United Kingdom. In 1969, Northern Ireland elected twelve members to the British parliament. One of them was Bernadette.

Bernadette often gave press conferences telling people about the problems in Northern Ireland.

"*A twenty-one-year-old Irish girl held the House of Commons spellbound today with a maiden speech of quiet eloquence and powerful emotion.*"
New York Times

Quick Notes

- Bernadette's father, John Devlin, was a carpenter.

- Bernadette made her first speech in parliament on April 22, 1969, one day before her twenty-second birthday.

- Bernadette published a book about her early life, *The Price of My Soul.*

Accomplishments

Within an hour of her arrival, Bernadette made her first speech in parliament. For more than twenty minutes, she told the other members just what was wrong with the way Northern Ireland was run. Sparing no details, she described what it was like to be poor and Catholic. Her speech made a great impression.

That summer, there were outbreaks of violence in Northern Ireland, with Protestants and Catholics fighting one another. Bernadette was often in the thick of the fighting, trying to protect Catholic families from the Protestants who were attacking their homes. The government of Northern Ireland accused her of encouraging the violence, and she was put on trial. Although Bernadette denied all charges, she was found guilty and sent to prison.

When Bernadette was released from jail four months later, she continued to speak her mind, both in parliament and outside it.

In 1969, Bernadette visited the large Irish community in New York City. She wanted support for the civil rights movement in Ireland.

January 30, 1972, has gone down in history as "Bloody Sunday." Although the government had forbidden demonstrations of any kind, six thousand people gathered in Londonderry to walk peacefully to the town center in a civil rights march. There, Bernadette was to address the crowd. The procession, which included women and children, started off in a relaxed mood. Suddenly, a small group of marchers, who wanted to cause trouble, began throwing stones at the British soldiers. The army opened fire, and thirteen marchers were killed.

Although Bernadette did not run in the next election, she remained a champion of Irish Catholics. Her work enraged many Protestants, however. Early one morning, when Bernadette, her husband, and their three children were still asleep, a group of Protestant **terrorists** broke into their home. Bernadette was shot fourteen times, and a bullet just missed her heart. Even this attack did not stop her.

Bernadette is still working for civil rights in Ireland. More than thirty years ago, she said, "We demand justice for all Irish." She is still saying it today.

BACKGROUNDER

Birmingham Six

In 1974, two bombs killed twenty-one people in England. Six Irish men were arrested, tried in court, and sent to jail for life. People all over Ireland were outraged, believing the Birmingham Six, as the prisoners were called, to be innocent. For sixteen years, protests and appeals failed to free them. For many Irish people, the Birmingham Six became a symbol of the injustices done to their country. In 1991, a judge finally released the prisoners and said the men had been jailed without proper evidence.

Bernadette and her daughter carrying the coffin of a fellow activist.

"I hadn't had a childhood at all. I hadn't been to school, I hadn't had enough food to grow properly. I had nothing."

Rigoberta Menchú

Guatemalan Human Rights Activist

Early Years

"I worked from when I was very small," Rigoberta told a journalist. She said she worked for fifteen hours a day, picking coffee berries beside her mother. The **overseer** reduced her pay if she rested for even a few minutes.

Rigoberta's home was high in the mountains in the village of Chimel in Guatemala, but her family seldom lived there. Their small patch of land could not grow enough crops to support them. They spent much of each year down on the coast, picking coffee or cotton on a big plantation. The pay was so low that all the children had to work, just to make ends meet.

Some people say that Rigoberta's life was not so hard. But this is how she describes it in her autobiography.

BACKGROUNDER

Descendants of an Ancient Civilization

Rigoberta and her family are descended from the Maya who lived in Central America long before any Europeans arrived. Hundreds of years ago, the Maya built huge cities and temples in the forests. They had an advanced system of mathematics, and they studied astronomy. Today, the Maya make up sixty to eighty percent of the population of Guatemala. Rigoberta's parents, Vicente and Juana Menchú, belonged to the Quiché group of Maya.

GULF OF MEXICO

CUBA

CARIBBEAN SEA

MEXICO

BELIZE
HONDURAS

GUATEMALA

NICARAGUA

EL SALVADOR

COSTA RICA

Developing Skills

In 1971, when Rigoberta was twelve, she went to work as a maid for a family in Guatemala City. She was treated even worse than on the plantation. Most days, all she had to eat were the leftovers from the family's plates. She slept on the floor on a straw mat next to the dog. After a year, she quit her job and returned home.

Rigoberta marching with other Maya-Quiché people in 1992.

As Rigoberta grew older, her life became even harder. Wealthy landowners wanted the land where the Maya lived and had their small farms. Some landowners sent soldiers to destroy the villages and drive out the Maya. When Rigoberta was a teenager, her father asked some workers' **unions** to help him prove that the land around Chimel belonged to the Quiché people. This action annoyed the landowners so much that they had him arrested.

Rigoberta's father was let out of prison a year later, but the landowner's guards kidnapped him soon afterward and hurt him so badly that he almost died. This made him all the more determined to fight back. He traveled from village to village, encouraging the people to oppose the landowners.

"Soldiers were kidnapping people all the time.... We'd hear of ten, fifteen people who had disappeared."

Rigoberta often traveled with her father. Like him, she became a member of the Committee of Peasant Unity, which by its Spanish initials is called CUC. In each village, she persuaded the people to join the CUC so that they could band together against the landowners.

Rigoberta knew that she was risking her life by organizing the villagers in this way. When she was twenty, soldiers kidnapped her younger brother. They tortured the boy for several days and then made the whole family watch as they killed him.

Soon afterward, Rigoberta's father and other **activists** took over the local radio station so they could tell the world about the torture and murder of thousands of Mayan villagers. To draw further attention to the way the Maya were being treated, they took over the Spanish Embassy in Guatemala City. They thought they would be safe there, because the government would not want the Spanish ambassador to be hurt. They were wrong. The army was called out, and soldiers threw grenades into the building. Everyone inside was killed, including Rigoberta's father.

A few months later, some soldiers captured and killed Rigoberta's mother. Rigoberta was left to carry on the struggle herself.

BACKGROUNDER

Rigoberta's Languages

Rigoberta grew up speaking Quiché, the most common Mayan language. When she became an activist, she learned three other Mayan languages so she could talk to people in other villages. Rigoberta later learned Spanish. Although Spanish is the official language of Guatemala, Rigoberta had not learned it as a child, because she never went to school.

In spite of the loss of her family, Rigoberta continues to fight against the oppression of the Mayan people.

BACKGROUNDER

The Guatemalan Civil War

In 1954, the elected president was **overthrown** by the army. The fighting continued for forty-two years. During this time, the cities were fairly peaceful, but the countryside was full of violence. The Maya suffered most. Any Maya who opposed the landowners was considered a rebel. Thousands of Maya were killed. Their villages were burned and their crops destroyed. In December 1996, a peace treaty was signed. As part of this treaty, the government promised to make life better for the Maya, and a group was appointed to look into the violence. In 1998, this group published a report that said that the army was guilty of most of the killings. A few days later, the bishop who had presented the report was murdered.

"I was a hunted woman.... The army were looking for me in various places."

Accomplishments

I n 1980, Rigoberta helped organize a **strike** of workers on the cotton and sugar plantations. The workers were demanding higher pay and better working conditions. Thousands of people joined the strike. As a leader of the CUC, Rigoberta also organized other protests. Soon, she heard that the army was looking for her.

Rigoberta hid at a friend's house, but she continued her political activities. One day, some soldiers spotted her on the street. She fled into a crowded church where she quickly knelt down like everyone else. The soldiers searched the church, but Rigoberta had let her hair down to hide her face, and she was not recognized. She realized that she was no longer safe in Guatemala. If the soldiers caught her, they would certainly kill her. They would also kill anyone found helping her. She left the country and went to live in Mexico.

A Catholic group helped Rigoberta get settled in Mexico. Another group arranged a trip to Europe so she could let people know about the terrible things that were happening in Guatemala. While she was in Europe, Rigoberta told her story to an author who wrote it into a book called I, Rigoberta Menchú. The book has been translated into a dozen languages and has been read throughout the world.

Rigoberta continued to do all she could to help her people. With others, she formed the National Committee for Reconciliation, which tried to stop the violence in Guatemala. For this and her other work for her people, she was awarded the Nobel Peace Prize in 1992. When the Guatemalan army chiefs heard she had won the prize, they were not pleased. Nor were many wealthy Guatemalans. They said she had been causing trouble, not promoting peace.

A large sum of money is always given with the Nobel Prize, and Rigoberta used it to set up a fund in memory of her father. Called the Vicente Menchú Foundation, the fund is used to promote human rights in Guatemala. Some of the money goes to educate the Quiché and other native Guatemalans.

Since then, Rigoberta has continued to work for better conditions for her people. She was pleased when the rebels and the government signed a peace treaty in 1996, but she knew it would take many years until people could forget the violence.

Quick Notes

- The Guatemalan Civil War was the longest conflict in Central America. At least 150,000 people died, and 50,000 more went missing.

- Rigoberta and her family are Catholic. Many Catholic priests and nuns sided with the Maya against the army.

- The Nobel Committee stated: "Rigoberta Menchú stands out as a vivid symbol of peace and reconciliation."

Rigoberta is interested in the problems of oppressed people around the world. She is seen here talking to a young girl from Burma in Southeast Asia.

"The education of the English boy was considered a much more serious matter than the education of the English boy's sister."

Emmeline Pankhurst

English Suffragette

Early Years

"What a pity she wasn't born a boy," said Emmeline's father one night when he thought she was asleep. Emmeline kept her eyes shut tight, but she was suddenly wide awake. Her father thought men were better than women!

Emmeline's parents considered themselves very advanced in their ways, and in comparison to most people in England at that time, they were. They were **activists**, who spent much of their time working for equal treatment of all people and they believed that women should be allowed to vote. Everyone should be treated fairly, they said. Yet in their house in Manchester, England, they favored their sons over their daughters.

There were eleven children in the family, and the boys went to better schools than the girls. Emmeline did not learn Latin or math at school. Instead, she was taught how to be "ladylike." That behavior was thought the most important thing for girls to know.

BACKGROUNDER

Early Activism

Emmeline's parents, Sophia and Robert, taught their children from an early age that all people were equal and to help those in need. One of Emmeline's first memories was of collecting money in a small bag at a rally to help **emancipated** slaves in the United States. Even as a child, Emmeline had heard many debates about the evils of slavery.

In 1862, the Emancipation Proclamation freed all slaves in the United States.

BACKGROUNDER

The Suffrage Movement

"Suffrage" means the right to vote in elections. A "suffragette" is a woman who tries to get women the right to vote. At the beginning of the nineteenth century, only a few people in England could vote. All of them were men, and most of them were property owners, people who owned their own homes. During the century, laws were passed giving the vote to more and more people. Each time, the suffragettes hoped that some women would be given the vote. By the end of the nineteenth century, although most English men had the right to vote, not one woman did.

Developing Skills

When Emmeline was twenty-one, she married a lawyer named Richard Pankhurst. Richard was much older than Emmeline, but they had the same interests. Both were strongly in favor of women's suffrage. Emmeline had been a suffragette since the age of fourteen, when her mother had taken her to a suffrage meeting. Richard had been an active suffrage worker for many years.

At the time of their marriage, the government in England promised to give the vote to many more people. This made Emmeline and Richard very hopeful. A few years later, the government kept its promise. It passed the Reform Bill of 1884, which added about two million people to those who were allowed to vote, but none of these people were women. Emmeline and Richard were furious.

Richard died in 1898, leaving Emmeline with four children to support. She took an office job to bring in some extra money. Meanwhile, she continued her suffrage work, helped by her eldest daughter, Christabel.

Emmeline and her daughter Christabel went to prison to bring public attention to the issue of votes for women.

In 1903, Emmeline, Christabel, and a few friends formed a suffrage group called the Women's Social and Political Union. The organization worked to get women the right to vote using only peaceful means. Emmeline had been brought up to be ladylike, and she believed in being polite. She started visiting members of parliament in their offices, explaining to them why women should be given the vote and asking them to help. Some members said they would support women's suffrage, but nothing happened.

Emmeline even talked to the prime minister. Still nothing happened. Clearly, the polite approach was not working. In 1905, Christabel and a friend went to an election meeting where an important politician was speaking. When he said, "Any questions?" they asked him, "Will the government give votes to women?" The politician did not reply, so they asked again ... and again. There was such an uproar that the two young women were thrown out of the hall. Outside, they were arrested for "creating a disturbance."

"We realized that, until it was forced to do so, the government would never give the vote to women."

The story was written up in the newspapers. At last, the media were taking notice! Emmeline realized that she had been using the wrong tactics. To get women the vote, she would have to stop behaving so politely. She would have to do things that would get the whole country talking.

Emmeline spoke to large groups to gain public support and to be noticed by politicians.

Quick Notes

- In 1909 and 1911, Emmeline visited the United States to encourage American women to fight for the right to vote.

- Two of Emmeline's daughters, Christabel and Sylvia, were very active in the suffrage movement. Both were imprisoned many times.

Accomplishments

In 1906, the suffragettes staged a big march in London. It encouraged many more women to join the movement. Led by Emmeline, the suffragettes continued to do everything possible to attract attention. They marched and sang in the streets. They waved flags in the faces of politicians, shouting, "Votes for Women!" Some of them even interrupted church services.

The police were ordered to stop the suffragettes, and sometimes they did so brutally. Emmeline was knocked unconscious during one march. Some women were arrested and sent to prison.

Emmeline was first sent to prison in 1908. At the jail, she was told to take off all her clothes and put on a prisoner's uniform. Emmeline had never undressed in public before, and she felt humiliated. However, she was determined to continue her work. A few months later, she was on the march again.

Since suffragettes were being imprisoned for doing nothing wrong, Emmeline thought they might as well break the law to get attention for their cause. She would not let her followers attack people, but she told them they could break windows and damage people's property. Many more suffragettes were arrested.

Emmeline's time in prison made her even more determined to work for women's suffrage.

The next time Emmeline was arrested, she went on a **hunger strike**. She became so weak from lack of food that the prison sent her home. As soon as she recovered, she was sent back to prison. During 1913, Emmeline was almost constantly on a hunger strike. Twelve times she was let out of prison, and twelve times she was sent back. Finally, she not only refused food, she also refused to drink anything. As usual, she was sent home to recover.

When World War I broke out in 1914, Emmeline stopped the suffrage campaign and put all her efforts into helping her country. The government responded by letting all suffragettes out of prison. Spurred on by Emmeline, many of them went to work in factories that made guns and other **munitions**.

In 1918, a suffrage law was at last passed giving women the vote. Although the law did not apply to all women, the suffragettes felt they had won a great battle. Ten years later, shortly before Emmeline died, all women in England were given the vote on the same terms as men.

. . . .

Emmeline collapsed from weakness after several hunger strikes.

BACKGROUNDER

Women's Suffrage in Other Countries

In 1907, some Norwegian women gained the vote. Canadian women gained the right to vote in national elections in 1918. In Germany, the date was 1919. In the United States, women could vote in national elections in 1920. Most English-speaking countries had women's suffrage by this time. In some other countries, such as France and Japan, women did not get the vote until after World War II, in the 1940s.

"No one who has not gone through the awful experience of the hunger strike can have any idea of how great that misery is."

More Women in Profile

Many other women around the world have rebelled for many causes.
The following pages list a few you may want to learn more about on your own.
Use the Suggested Reading list to learn more about these and other women rebels.

1820–1906
Susan B. Anthony
American Suffragette

Susan was the leader of the women's suffrage movement in the United States. She was arrested in 1872 for voting illegally (by dropping a voting paper into a ballot box), but she was never imprisoned like Emmeline Pankhurst. Susan believed that women should stop wearing long skirts so that they could have a freer and more active life. For a whole year, she wore a "bloomer costume" of baggy pants. She was often ridiculed for her actions, but later in life, people began to accept her ideas.

Susan B. Anthony

1844–1934
Catherine Breshkovsky
Russian Revolutionary

Born into a wealthy family at the time when the **tsars** still ruled Russia, Catherine saw that life in her country was very unfair. Millions of people lived in conditions that were close to slavery. Catherine was determined to set them free. She traveled from village to village, encouraging the peasants to rebel against the government. She was arrested and imprisoned for many years. Catherine's activities helped bring about the Russian Revolution of 1917, which ended the rule of the tsars. She was known as the Mother of the Revolution. Yet she did not approve of the communist government that took over after the revolution, and she later left Russia.

1879–1907
Ch'iu Chin
Chinese Revolutionary

Ch'iu was one of the earliest of China's revolutionaries. She dared to speak out against the powerful emperors who ruled China, and she formed secret societies to try and **overthrow** them. Ch'iu was captured and tortured, but she refused to confess to any crimes. She was then beheaded. The Chinese honor her as one of their great heroes.

c. 1955–
Phoolan Devi
India's "Bandit Queen"

The leader of a gang of outlaws, Phoolan is a hero to many because she fought against the unfair treatment of Indian women. Many people feared her, because she robbed the rich and was

Phoolan Devi

said to have killed some of her enemies. Tired of being hunted by the police, Phoolan gave herself up in 1983 and was imprisoned. In 1994, she was pardoned and let out of jail. Later, she was elected a member of parliament.

1865–1927
Kageyama Hideko
Japanese Socialist

Kageyama is a hero in Japan because of her efforts to make life better for working women and their children. She and her mother opened a school for underprivileged children, but it was closed by the government. Kageyama's response was to try to form a new government. She did not succeed and was jailed for a year. Even so, she never gave up her struggle. She started a **socialist** magazine, which spoke out on behalf of women, laborers, and peasant farmers.

1870–1919
Rosa Luxemburg
Polish-German Revolutionary

Rosa was a **socialist** who led workers' revolts in Poland and Germany, trying to get the workers better conditions. During World War I, she organized the Spartacus Party, which later became the German Communist party. In 1919, the party led a general **strike** in the city of Berlin. It was brutally put down, and Rosa was shot.

1949–

Ingrid Newkirk

British Animal Rights Activist

After moving to the United States, Ingrid became one of the founders of PETA (People for the Ethical Treatment of Animals). PETA wants to stop animals from being used in experiments. Ingrid says it is both cruel and unnecessary to make a rabbit blind just to see if a shampoo, for example, will harm people's eyes. She says that animals have the same basic rights as people.

1955–

Joice Nhongo

Zimbabwean Guerrilla Fighter

At the age of eighteen, Joice ran away from home to join the "boys in the bush" who were fighting to free their country from British rule. She became one of the most famous fighters in the **guerrilla** army. After Zimbabwe became an independent country, Joice was elected to parliament.

1913–

Rosa Parks

American Civil Rights Activist

Born in Alabama, Rosa made history in 1955 when she refused to give up her bus seat when a white man demanded it. At the time, buses in the American South were segregated, with different sections for African Americans and white travelers. Rosa was sitting in the

Rosa Parks

central section, where African Americans were allowed to sit, as long as no whites wanted those seats. Her refusal to give up her seat launched the civil rights movement, which brought many improvements for African Americans.

1882–1947

Huda Sharawi

Egyptian Activist

In 1919, when Egypt was a British **colony**, Huda led more than three hundred women in a march against the British. She also protested against Egypt's unequal treatment of women, by not wearing a veil across her face and head. This was considered so shocking that her husband divorced her. She fought for women's education and opened Egypt's first girls' school.

1831–1903

Emily Stowe
Canadian Suffragette and Doctor

Emily founded Canada's first suffrage group to get Canadian women the vote. She was also the first Canadian woman to practice as a doctor. By demanding the same rights for women as men, Emily shocked many people, but she drew attention to women's needs. By the time she died, there was a strong suffrage movement in Canada.

Emily Stowe

c. 1820–1913

Harriet Tubman
American Hero of the Underground Railroad

Harriet rebelled against slavery. She was born a slave in Maryland, but she escaped and made her way to Canada along the secret route known as the Underground Railroad. During the following years, she became a "conductor" on the Underground Railroad, helping other slaves escape. Each time she did, she risked her life, but she was never caught.

1909–1943

Simone Weil
French Socialist and Philosopher

Trained as a teacher, Simone was fired from school after school because she was viewed as a dangerous **socialist**. Teachers were expected not to join protest marches in the streets, as Simone did. She marched to demand higher wages and better conditions for the workers. She got jobs in factories and on farms to find out how working people lived. Today, Simone is considered one of the most important philosophers of the twentieth century.

Glossary

activist: someone who works hard for a cause

colony: a region ruled by another country

communism: a system in which all property and goods are owned by the government and are supposed to be shared equally by all people

deforestation: cleared of trees and forests

downtrodden: oppressed and badly treated

emancipated: to be set free

firebrand: a person who causes unrest

guerrilla: an independent soldier fighting against a regular army

hunger strike: when someone refuses food as a form of protest

left wing: a radical or socialist political group

munitions: war equipment, including weapons, ammunition, and military supplies

overseer: someone who supervises workers

overthrow: to remove from power by force

racism: treating people differently—usually unfairly—because of their race

refugee: a person seeking protection from war, natural disaster, or persecution

republic: a country where the highest power is an elected official, not royalty

right wing: means different things in different countries; in this case it is a conservative political group that supports the power of the wealthy

seedlings: a young plant, usually raised from a seed

socialist: a person who believes that the community, not a few individuals, should own and manage land and money

strike: the refusal by employees to work until their demands are met

terrorist: someone who uses violence for political reasons

tsars: the powerful rulers of Russia before the Russian Revolution

unions: groups of workers who unite to form politically active groups

Suggested Reading

Forbes, Malcolm. *Women Who Made a Difference*. New York: Simon and Schuster, 1990.

Fraser, Antonia. *Heroes and Heroines*. London: Weidenfeld & Nicolson, 1980.

Golemba, Beverley. *Lesser-Known Women*. Boulder: Rienner, 1992.

Hacker, Carlotta. *Great African Americans in History*. Niagara-on-the-Lake: Crabtree, 1997.

Ibarruri, Dolores. *They Shall Not Pass: The Autobiography of La Pasionaria*. London: Lawrence & Wischart, 1966.

Menchú, Rigoberta. *I, Rigoberta Menchú*. London: Verso, 1984.

Nadelson, Regina. *Who Is Angela Davis?* New York: Wyden, 1972.

Pankhurst, Emmeline. *My Own Story*. Westport, Connecticut: Greenwood Press, [c. 1914], 1985.

Raven, Susan, and Alison Weir. *Women of Achievement*. New York: Harmony, 1981.

Saari, Peggy. *Prominent Women of the Twentieth Century*. Detroit: UXL, 1986.

Index

1 2 3 4 5 6 7 8 9 0 Printed in Canada 8 7 6 5 4 3 2 1 0 9